JUST HOLD ME

JUST HOLD ME

EMBRACED BY THE SAVIOR'S LOVE

DON H. STAHELI

DESERET
BOOK

SALT LAKE CITY, UTAH

Artwork on pages 4 and 70 © Intellectual Reserve, Inc.
Artwork on pages 10 and 28 © Walter Rane
Artwork on pages 16, 21, and 36 © Robert Barrett
Artwork on pages 48 and 77 © Simon Dewey
All artwork used by permission.

Visit us at deseretbook.com

Library of Congress Cataloging-in-Publication Data

Staheli, Don H.
  Just hold me : embraced by the Savior's love / Don H. Staheli.
      p.   cm.
  ISBN 1-59038-357-5 (hardbound : alk. paper)
  1. Christian life—Mormon authors. I. Title.
  BX8656.S73 2004
  248.4'89332—dc22

                                                              2004014226

Printed in Mexico   18961
R. R. Donnelley, Reynosa, Mexico

10   9   8   7   6   5   4   3   2

With appreciation to Sheri Dew,
Cathy Chamberlain, Jana Erickson, and
Richard Peterson of Deseret Book

The Staheli Family Motto

In essentials, unity;

in nonessentials, liberty;

in all things, charity.

MELANCTHON

CONTENTS

For I know that such will sorrow for the calamity

of the house of Israel; yea, they will sorrow for

the destruction of this people; they will sorrow

that this people had not repented that they might

have been clasped in the arms of Jesus.

MORMON 5:11

The Well-Timed Embrace

Early one morning, in a few moments of grateful reflection, I considered the many ways in which we feel the embrace of loving people, of a precious life, and, especially, of our longsuffering Lord Jesus Christ. Memories came and formed themselves into brief vignettes. With each image came an increased sense of joy and warmth, like being swaddled in a thousand hugs. Reminiscences of:

- ✦ Basking in Mom's caring smile, her tender touch, and a plate of her gumdrop bars. She was always there when we got home
- ✦ Enjoying the distinctive smell of Grandma

and Grandpa's house and receiving their hugs and kisses when we came and went

* Delighting in a tail-wagging mutt, with a lolling tongue, awaiting my exit from the school bus
* Kneeling in spartan missionary quarters, enfolded in the arms of the Spirit, knowing my Savior and knowing why I was there
* Experiencing hopes and possibilities I'd never imagined while being embraced by a beautiful girl with whom I was falling in love
* Being swarmed with hugs from five wonderful children, the oldest not yet eight, and each one a little clone of goodness and light
* Being encircled in the arms of a big man/ good friend, who wasn't afraid to say, "I love you."
* Speaking to a congregation of one or a thousand people who needed to know they were understood

Each of these and a lifetime of similar experiences have provided me the feeling of being totally embraced, in a full-body hug that includes the soul and that has propped me up, warmed me up, and left me better off.

So goes the life of embracing and being embraced. Some of us are lucky enough to receive such comfort often and without any obvious merit; we have been fattened on a diet of acceptance. Others are deprived, seldom or never blessed by such nurturing moments or relationships, no matter how much they might be desired or deserved. Sometimes only heaven can provide the necessary emotional nutrition.

Studies of newborns confirm that to be held is a fundamental human need. The warmth and acceptance transferred to the infant by its early caregivers is essential not only to its emotional but physical development. And that need never goes away. As infants, children, young adults, or grownups, we crave and require physical manifestations that we are accepted, loved, and valued. Such unconditional love from some other being is basic to our happiness.

Knowing this, and seeking to generate an emotional response from their audience, movie makers

Detail from *The Second Coming*, Harry Anderson

often depict the timely embrace. The most evocative moments in a film are those where a comrade-in-arms cradles his expiring buddy, a star-crossed or reconciled couple finally finds love and acceptance in each other's arms, a child finds security and safety in the loving hug of a parent, or the long-lost wanderer returns to the welcoming embrace of affectionate kin. The tighter the squeeze and the longer the embrace, the more poignant the scene.

What is there about a hug, about being held close to the bosom of one whose affection we crave, that means so much to us? Why is it that to be enfolded in the arms of a concerned other proffers so much comfort and sustaining warmth? Perhaps we can gain some insight by examining a few heart-warming scenes from the movies and discovering in them something of what we desire in our own relationships.

But the warm and tender embrace is not just the stuff of fiction. We will also explore some powerful examples from the scriptures and from the lives of real people. Through these we will come to know that the loving arms of the Savior are open wide to receive us—that when no one else seems to be around, when others do not appear to understand or even pay attention to our need for a hug, He is there. That is the assurance provided by Mormon, who testified that if all the world should abandon us, "if the heavens gather blackness, and all the elements combine to hedge up the way; and above all, if the very jaws of hell shall gape open the mouth wide after [us]" (Doctrine & Covenants 122:7), we can still be "clasped in the arms of Jesus" (Mormon 5:11).

HOLD ME

One of the great western dramas ever filmed is the wonderful movie *Shane*, starring Alan Ladd as a handsome, charismatic gunfighter who drifts into the Teton Valley in the hope of finding a new life away from the violence he has known. This proves to be a difficult task. Conflict between the defenseless homesteaders and violent men employed by the powerful rancher who has previously laid claim to the open range results in a dramatic showdown. In spite of his desire to avoid it, Shane is drawn into the conflict and ends up using his deadly skill to rid the valley of the ruthless men who oppose encroaching civilization.

A sub-plot in the story is the relationship between Shane and Marian, the wife of Joe Starrett, the homesteader for whom Shane is working. The pretty, pioneer woman has settled into a routine of work and hardship devoid of excitement or romance, and she finds something irresistable in the gallant and somewhat mysterious Shane. Marian is a virtuous woman and faithful wife, but she is momentarily intrigued by the alluring stranger.

In one pivotal scene she and Shane are alone in the main room of the cabin. Her husband and son have gone off to prepare for bed. Marian stands close to Shane, who is seated at the table where she has been tending to his latest wounds. Just then the boy calls, and she leaves the room with the expectation of a quick return. By the time she comes back, Shane, sensing her feelings and seeking to prevent anything inappropriate from happening, has left the house, and the distracted farmer's wife stands watching dreamily out the doorway after this intriguing man.

Then the door of the bedroom opens, and Joe discovers his wife gazing at their retreating guest.

Somewhat naively, Joe says to his wife, "What's the matter, honey?" The good woman turns and almost runs back to reality and the solid safety to be found in the arms of her plain but noble husband. "Hold me," she implores. "Don't say anything, just hold me— tight."

Just hold me and remind me of what I have, was her unspoken plea. No need to articulate. Such feelings can hardly be put into words anyway. Just take me into your powerful arms and bring home my heart.

In much the same manner, when as the world calls to us, should we drift a bit toward the siren song or even fall headlong into the grasp of evil hands, we can come to our senses and run to the sheltering arms of the Savior. He will speak without naivete when he inquires, "What's the matter, dear daughter (or son)? I am here and willing to help." And speak He will, as He said, "whether by mine own voice or by the voice of my servants, it is the same" (Doctrine and Covenants 1:38). Through the sweet whisperings of the Spirit, as a voice in our mind or a feeling in our heart, or by the counsel of a caring person who sees and

His Father Rejoiced, Alma the Younger, Walter Rane

understands our plight, the guidance will come. Comfort and reassurance will arrive, and we can find safety and love in His waiting arms.

The experience of Alma the Younger bears powerful witness of the effectiveness of the Lord's outreach. As the rebellious young man was reined in by angelic remonstrance, he rapidly came to a vivid sense of his own guilt and shame. Following a period of intense self-reproach, he yielded to the entreaty of his Lord and great became his joy. "I could remember my pains no more;" he testified. "I was harrowed up by the memory of my sins no more. And oh, what joy, and what marvelous light I did behold; yea, my soul was filled with joy as exceeding as was my pain!" (Alma 36:19–20). In answer to the prayers of his righteous father and with a knowledge of young Alma's Saul-to-Paul potential to do as much good as he had been doing bad, the Savior willingly received the repentant boy and fully embraced his sincere desire to go forward, shielded by his loving Lord from the threats of the evil one. He will do the same for us.

Though it may seem that our own displacement

from the right way has put us too far out to be reclaimed, it is not so. Not for anyone. If it is lost we feel, then we can listen to the voices calling for our return and move in their direction.

Our Savior knows perfectly well what it is to suffer unyielding temptation. He felt the very eyes of Satan focused upon Him, as the destroyer was bent on His demise. He knows what it's like to be mired in the sinkhole of self-hate, to be weighed down with the heavy burden of sin. In His ordeal in Gethsemane He went to all these places and infinitely more, to unimaginable realms of fear and guilt and despair, and then He returned as clean as when He went in, fully prepared to redeem us from anyplace we might stray. His arms are open and He will respond with warmth and love. He won't say a word to condemn us; we have plenty of those for ourselves. He will only offer His embrace.

TIGHTER

T he classic movie *West Side Story* is a tragic
screenplay of hope and hopelessness, of big city
life and death. As the plot reaches its climax,
handsome Bernardo is dead. Tony has killed him in a
gang fight gone wrong. The other gang members are
hiding and plotting revenge and how to protect their
concrete turf, but Tony is overwhelmed with remorse
and guilt. He has slain the brother of his new love,
Maria. How can he make things right? In agony, Tony
comes to Maria to express his sorrow and declare his
plan to go to the police. Beside herself with grief,
confused at her love for an enemy of her people, and
fearful of involving the law, Maria cries, "No!"

In desperation and agony, Tony declares, "Whatever you want, I'll do!"

"Hold me," pleads Maria, as she collapses into his arms. "Tighter."

All she could think to ask was that he hold her. Tighter, and maybe I can keep you with me. Tighter, and your embrace will shut out the harshness of the world. Tighter, and all the ugliness and hatred may disappear. Just hold me, and love will rule our universe.

In this demanding and frightening world we are besieged with terrifying images—of war, natural disasters, and personal calamity. We see the sword and feel the terror as Moses predicted, and witness, as he said, the destruction of "both the young man and the virgin, the suckling also with the man of gray hairs" (Deuteronomy 32:25). No one is immune from the pressures and risks of latter-day life.

In Satan's attempt to thwart the plan of happiness he has succeeded in causing many to rush violently, like the swine described in Matthew 8:32, down "a steep place" to the waters of destruction, without regard for whom they might step on as they go. In the wake of this mad and meaningless race are left the bruised and broken bodies and minds of the innocent who just couldn't get out of the way in time. It is so difficult in our day to avoid being damaged in the headlong dash for worldly pleasure and gain. Even though we know there is plenty for everyone, it is hard not to be trampled by those who think they will only have enough when they have taken ours, too.

Children are tragically harmed by the abuser, who can think of nothing but acting out his or her evil compulsions. Fragile egos, like thin ice, are easily cracked by people who would thoughtlessly tread on the still developing personalities of those of us who are not so self-assured. Sometimes the worst of it comes from those who profess to love us and surely ought to know better. To such we have opened our hearts and thus become more vulnerable to their betrayal.

But even in our utmost distress the Redeemer stands ready to rescue us, His children. He will do for us what Martha knew He would do for her. "I know," she said to her dear friend, "that even now, whatsoever

Lazarus Come Forth, Robert Barrett

thou wilt ask of God, God will give it thee" (John 11:22).

Though her beloved brother, Lazurus, had been laid in his tomb and she was almost inconsolable due to grief, the Master brought her hope. Martha would yet know the embrace of this special member of her family. Through the power of God and in furtherance of the Savior's ministry, Lazurus would be raised from the dead and made lively and whole. The good of his life would be returned to those who needed him, and he and they would again share the joys so deeply desired.

For us, the dead for whom we long will probably not be returned. The harsh realities of life are unlikely to be completely erased. Nonetheless, we can find peace in the knowledge that, whether in this life or the next, all will be made well. The sustaining arms of the Lord will give us strength to endure what He chooses not to remove. "And now it came to pass that the burdens which were laid upon Alma and his brethren were made light; yea, the Lord did strengthen them that they could bear up their burdens with ease, and they did submit cheerfully and with patience to all the will of the Lord" (Mosiah 24:15). We may become impatient with His seemingly late response to our requests for relief, but we must never doubt that He will surely come, as He has promised. And when we know He is with us, we will soon become aware that He was never actually gone.

Our very real Savior offers Himself to us in the same manner as the fictional Tony did to his storybook love. "Whatever you want, I'll do!" He anxiously awaits our response. Plead with Him to hold you, to embrace you in His love, and bring to you respite from the terror and escape from the pain. We have this assurance: "Now the God of hope [will] fill you with all joy and peace" (Romans 15:13).

And They Wept

I n the most critical moments of life we seek the warm embrace of someone who loves us. This is not something dreamed up by the movie studios or simply a contemporary, psychological coping device. It is an age-old longing to which even the most cynical or calloused of us can easily relate. The scriptures contain many such helping, healing, tender encounters.

Recall the moving reunion between Jacob and his estranged twin brother, Esau, the eldest by minutes. The conflict between the two brothers reached its apex when Jacob somewhat deceptively received the birthright blessing of his father, Isaac, to which Esau was technically entitled by virtue of their birth order.

Filled with anger and plotting revenge, Esau planned to kill Jacob.

"And Esau hated Jacob because of the blessing wherewith his father blessed him: and Esau said in his heart, The days of mourning for my father are at hand; then will I slay my brother Jacob.

"And these words of Esau her elder son were told to Rebekah" (Genesis 27:41–42).

Rebekah, mother of the boys, warned Jacob, who then left to go live with his Uncle Laban until Esau could cool off. More than fourteen years later, Jacob determined to return home with his now large family. This meant meeting Esau again, which was still a frightening prospect for Jacob, who was unaware of his twin bother's current state of mind regarding the birthright blessing affair. As he got close to home, Jacob's fears were not lessened. He saw Esau coming with 400 men!

"And [Jacob] passed over before them, and bowed himself to the ground seven times, until he came near to his brother.

"And Esau ran to meet him, and embraced him,

Esau and Jacob Embracing, Robert Barrett

and fell on his neck, and kissed him: and they wept" (Genesis 33:3–4).

We can only imagine the relief Jacob experienced as he received not the wrath but the forgiveness, kindness, and affection of his former enemy. As they held one another, they wept for the joy of reconciliation and family unity. One heartfelt embrace, and fear was gone, past anger dissipated, and peace and love restored.

Many of us fear approaching the Savior and seeking His embrace. Dwelling on our failures and feeling guilty or unworthy, we wrongfully assume He would have no interest in us, or we imagine that he might entirely reject us. Having experienced such rejection from others and recalling that we have rejected those who have offended us, we suppose He will do likewise. Because we can't bear the thought of His spurning our approach, be it ever so humble and contrite, we withdraw from Him, isolated in our anguish and left to yearn for the tender acceptance of our beloved Master.

His entreaties, however, belie such a notion of divine rejection. "Come unto me," He said to "all . . .

that labour and are heavy laden, and I will give you rest" (Matthew 11:28). "Draw near unto me and I will draw near unto you; seek me diligently and ye shall find me; ask, and ye shall receive; knock, and it shall be opened unto you" (Doctrine &Covenants 88:63). How many times and how many ways does He have to offer His embrace before we trust in His sincerity? "How oft would I have gathered you as a hen gathereth her chickens under her wings, . . . yea, how oft would I have gathered you as a hen gathereth her chickens, and ye would not" (3 Nephi 10:5). He would, but we wouldn't. We can change that. We can now surrender to His love and accept His offer of shelter under His protecting wing. It is His prayer that we will. It is our prayers that will bring us there.

Even from a Great Way Off

J esus didn't have the luxury of computer-aided animation, but His ability to stimulate the imaginations of His listeners through examples and metaphors was unequaled. Moreover, He knew the thoughts and the feelings of his listeners' hearts, and He "taught them as one having authority" (Matthew 7:29), which made for a powerful presentation.

His parable of the prodigal son is particularly rich in meaning and emotion. The twenty-one verses penned by Luke in recording the Savior's words carry lesson after lesson about greed, desperation, remorse, humility, and forgiveness, not to mention the unconditional love of a father. Each of us can relate to at least one of the three people in the story: the reckless younger brother, the faithful eldest son, or the merciful father.

In a manner consistent with the culture of that time and place, the young man in the parable exercises his option to take his inheritance early and strike out on his own. He has no trouble finding those who are anxious to provide the revelry he seeks in exchange for his newfound wealth. He lives high on the proverbial hog until his money runs out and he finds himself literally dwelling with the pigs.

When the wayward youth is finally driven to his senses (hunger is a powerful reminder to boys!), he aims toward home, hoping for at least some form of acceptance, if not forgiveness. Jesus paints a moving picture of his arrival. In fact, the scene is almost painfully tender. The father is said to have seen his wayward son "when [the boy] was yet a great way off," which suggests the heartbroken father had not given up but was *watching* for his precious son's return. Then, not content to wait for the prodigal's arrival, the father "ran, and fell on his neck, and kissed him" (Luke 15:20).

Home at last and received again into the embrace of a loving father. Accepted still as a son and not as a servant. He had spent his monetary inheritance; it was gone and never to be retrieved as such. But he still had emotional money in the bank with his father. He might have used up his cash, but the currency of love had not run out, and this was now being freely spent in his behalf by a father indescribably joyful over his son's hoped-for return.

As heartwarming as the story is, it has application beyond the family it describes. The truth is, despite our straying from the way of righteousness, regardless of how we may have distanced ourselves from God, our Father/Redeemer will come to us and, in a manner as real as any father's embrace, will have compassion and encompass us in His fervent welcome back. He is watching and waiting for our return. If we move toward Him, He will come out to greet us.

It is unfortunate, but we see the story of the prodigal son being played out today in the behavior of

His Father Had Compassion, *The Prodigal Son*, Walter Rane

those young and old who feel that the world owes them something more than they appear to be gaining through the routine of daily life. Seeking an elusive fulfillment and to feed appetites that can never be satisfied, husbands stray from sacred vows, wives are stressed and distracted, sons rebel and follow forbidden paths, and daughters depart the teachings of sorrowing parents. Tragic are the losses of those who go so far that the family reunion is long and hard in coming.

In the parable, the boy drifted away to near ruin and then, recalling the goodness of his previous position, reversed his course and returned, to be fully embraced in the happiness of his home. If we have strayed, perhaps now is the time to return. If we feel that Heavenly Father has moved away from us, then we must know that He can see us "a great way off," and can close the gap in an instant. Time and distance, whether physical or spiritual, pose no obstacle for Him. He only awaits a sign of our repentant willingness, for He will "force no man to heav'n" (*Hymns*, no. 240). As we seek Him and wait upon Him, His

Spirit will fall upon us as though we were literally enfolded in His sweet embrace.

Let us not put off the day of our return, thinking we can live indefinitely on the husks of unholy behavior. Do not let it be said of us as it was of the Nephites: "O ye fair ones, how could ye have departed from the ways of the Lord! O ye fair ones, how could ye have rejected that Jesus, who stood with open arms to receive you!" (Mormon 6:17).

Each of us is numbered among the "fair ones" in the family of God. Oh, how our Father yearns for our return. Perhaps we'll come home a bit disheveled by the burdens of mortality, but He will accept us as we are. We must forsake our pride and self-declared independence and yield to our longing for the warm hearth of His heavenly abode. No older sibling will resent our homecoming. The welcome will be universal. "Joy shall be in heaven" (Luke 15:7), and the Eldest will be the first to suggest we be honored. In fact, He will allot to us equally, if we have not deliberately squandered our portion of the inheritance which only He merits, but in which all who will may share alike.

Such is the promise to each who accepts the invitation to come home to the open arms of the Father and His Son. We can enjoy the wonderful embrace of God—be we the one who was "ever with me" or the one who "was lost, and is found." That can be our blessing here and now; and when this life is over, we will bask in eternal joy at the foot of His throne (see Doctrine & Covenants 59:23).

Satan's Embrace

In stark contrast to the tenderness of the heavenly embrace of Jesus is the awful grasp of Satan. One being could not be more different from another than these two. Though they share a thread of commonality in their origins—both highly favored of God—they could not have walked a more divergent path. Jesus Christ offers to hold us in the arms of His love. Since the day of His selfless, loving declaration, "Here am I, send me" (Abraham 3:27), He has stood over us, arms outstretched in both a protective and receptive mode, defending, healing, comforting, and gathering in those who would look to Him and live.

But what kind of embrace does Satan offer?

Some of the early Nephites, prior to their redemption, felt Satan's hold and "were encircled about by the bands of death, and the chains of hell, and an everlasting destruction did await them" (Alma 5:7). Lucifer had them in his awful clutches. He was not just the author of temptation, one who might simply try to tickle their fancy for vice or put a burr under the saddle of their otherwise comfortable lives. Having forfeited his eternal blessings, Satan became, and remains, a mean and evil being who takes satisfaction only in our misery, "for he seeketh that all men might be miserable like unto himself" (2 Nephi 2:27). Consider the Lord's frightening description of the tools Satan employs to capture and enslave us: "[His] is an iron yoke, it is a strong band; they are the very handcuffs, and chains, and shackles, and fetters of hell" (Doctrine & Covenants 123:8).

What greater contrast can one imagine: to be "encircled about by the bands of death, and . . . everlasting destruction" (Alma 5:7) versus being "encircled about eternally in the arms of his love" (2 Nephi 1:15).

And how does Satan bind us? Some seem to go willingly, as they mindlessly follow the philosophy of the natural man or woman. "And behold, others he flattereth away, and telleth them there is no hell; and he saith unto them: I am no devil, for there is none— and thus he whispereth in their ears, until he grasps them with his awful chains, from whence there is no deliverance" (2 Nephi 28:22). The results are the same and none of them pleasant to imagine or easy to endure.

If the natural woman or man has gotten the better of us and we are spiraling down into the pain-ridden pits of the devil's domain, a literal hell on earth, then we must do all within our power to call upon God and reach up to accept His outstretched, saving hand. As quickly as we reject our self-destructive behavior and look to Him to bind up the wounds and fill in the stress cracks that have developed in our personalities and performances, He will draw us into His loving embrace.

Christ Walking on Water with Peter, Robert Barrett

By listening to the quiet but wise still small voice of the Holy Spirit, by reading the scriptures, and by paying diligent heed to the inspired counsel of our authorized priesthood leaders, we will be schooled in the art of discernment—the ability to tell evil from good. By consistently choosing the right, we will be enabled to quickly shake off the soft threads of iniquity that would wrap around us until they have woven themselves into gnarly links only heaven can break. It is wise to think carefully and to continually evaluate the fibers of everyday experience, which are being woven into the fabric of our lives. Only those things which are "virtuous, lovely, or of good report or praiseworthy" will lead us to be "honest, true, chaste, [and] benevolent" (see Articles of Faith 1:13).

Popularity in the world could never be the sole measure of acceptability to God. Indeed, the more we fashion our lives after the ways of men, the greater the chance we will be found wearing the useless garb of the emperor of evil. Trendy lifestyles may bring momentary pleasure, satisfy our vanity, enhance our social status, and bring adulation from those who fear or would flatter us, but the Lord can see through such, and our worldly attire will be seen for what it is when the time comes for an honest evaluation of our spiritual wardrobe.

Thank heaven the embrace of Jesus will wrest us from the sticky web of Satan. As we are taken into His arms, we can go from "the pains of a damned soul," "in the gall of bitterness," to a joy "so exquisite and sweet" it defies expression (Alma 36:16, 18, 21). Falling into the outstretched arms of the Lord, we are rescued from "the chains, and shackles, and fetters of hell" (Doctrine & Covenants 123:8) and embraced by that sweet peace and safety of which the Savior spoke: "Peace I leave with you, my peace I give unto you: not as the world giveth, give I unto you. Let not your heart be troubled, neither let it be afraid" (John 14:27).

To pry apart the clutching fingers of our enraged enemy and break his painful grasp, we must humble ourselves, cease our destructive behavior, call upon God, and believe in His ultimate love and kindness. Then, as Aaron promised King Lamoni (and the covenant holds true for us today), "shalt thou receive the hope which thou desirest" (Alma 22:16).

If we are to escape Satan's clutches, we must act with all haste, before the cords of evil cut off the circulation and our spiritual limbs are numbed and no longer able to respond. Only Jesus can unlash us from the mast of Satan's sinking vessel ere it is swallowed up in the depths and we go haplessly down with the ship of wickedness, following the captain of lies to his place of dark exile.

As our hearts are cleared of evil desires, our souls will be quickly and amply filled with hope for our eternal well-being. Such hope brings peace and lasting joy, the value of which exceeds all earthly possessions. Then, as though a downy mantle of love were draped across our shoulders, the chill of Satan's rude blast is forgotten, and we are comfortably wrapped in the warm embrace of Jesus Christ.

A Rock in My Shoe

A common occurence once gave me some insight as to the insidious nature of sin and just how easily evil can sneak into our lives and bring us misery. In an instant I realized why even a little sin is intolerable to the Lord, who desires our undiluted happiness.

I got a pebble in my shoe.

Pausing on the sidewalk, I assumed a one-legged, flamingo-like stance and attempted to untie my shoe without sitting down. It was an awkward position, and I struggled to keep my balance by shifting my weight and hopping about. I think humans are not well-suited to bending over and taking off a shoe while perched on one foot.

All of these gyrations were necessitated by the boulder that had somehow worked its way into my shoe and was making each stride an exercise in agony. How such a huge piece of granite had gained access to the inside of my wing-tipped footwear was a mystery. But regardless of how it came to get in, it was huge and now causing great pain and making it impossible to walk another step. Thus, the necessity of stopping to fidget with the shoelace, take off the shoe, and remove the offending hunk of gravel.

When I finally got the shoe off, I turned it upside down and shook it. Nothing fell out. Where was the boulder? I inserted my hand into the shoe and felt around carefully. I couldn't feel anything of substance until, wait, there seemed to be something lodged in the soft insole. More probing yielded a tiny grain of aggregate not bigger than a few combined particles of sand. The boulder was nowhere to be found, just this little pebble. What had seemed like a rock big enough to cripple an elephant was only a minuscule morsel of stone. How could such a tiny thing cause so much discomfort?

It doesn't take much to slow us down or even bring us to a halt. Goliath (though the stone was not in his shoe, but in his forehead!) learned this lesson from a young David. The progress of even the most powerful and promising can be brought up short with the intrusion of just a small amount of foreign material in the wrong place at the wrong time.

Sin will have a similar effect upon us. It will cause us to slacken our pace, even more quickly than a pebble in our shoe. A small amount of sin, not much in comparison with all the good that we account to ourselves, can make it painful to keep going or can stop our forward progress altogether. It doesn't seem to matter how big we are or how important or how well developed our spiritual musculature, if the gravel of evil and the grit of sin get in where they don't belong, they will create enough pain to stop even the best of us.

When that happens, we must pause in our efforts, bend or even better kneel down, and remove the offending source of spiritual pain. Sometimes this is accomplished with the help of others and always within the protecting arms of the Savior, who will shield and protect us until we are able to regain our balance, tie life back on like a comfortable shoe, and stride off to meet whatever the hard packed pathway of mortality might bring to us next. When (not if!) we pick up another "sinstone," the well-practiced process of removal will work every time to get us comfortably back under way. There is nothing like a clean shoe or a clear conscience to make our walk more pleasant and easier.

HIS EMBRACE BRINGS WHOLENESS

B y virtue of our mortality and the divine design of our earthly curriculum, we are susceptible to evil influence and must resist at all times its alluring fascination. Lucifer is perfectly attuned to the chords that would resonate with the baser elements of our nature, and he will orchestrate a score of appealing sounds and sights that will attract the attention of all who choose to listen to His wicked song. The more resistant we are to his wiles, the more intense and individualized will be his probings. Like water seeping in where it is not dammed, he will explore the areas of our least resistance and, if we do not seal the leaky spots, flood our souls with thoughts and behavior that will distance us from God and His righteousness.

There are points of weakness in each of our lives. We are all vulnerable in one way or another. Each of us has areas in our psyche that nature has not fortified or that opportunity has not graced with wholeness. Some of the gaps we can tolerate without closing. We can just live with them in relative happiness and chronic incompleteness. Others we can fill in a manner that will benefit ourselves and those around us, lessening our pettiness and envy, and increasing our capacity to do good. But Satan would lead us in a selfish pursuit of what he would like us to view as entitlements. He would have us pursue feel-good personal satisfactions and do so with a reckless lack of concern for others and a foolish disregard of the consequences.

If we surrender to his way of thinking, Lucifer will gladly provide no end of opportunity to indulge our selfish desires and sinful longings. For the moment, such pursuits will seem justified and well-deserved, but in the end sin produces no lasting contentment, only remorse and a hunger that can never be satisfied.

Listening to the seductive song emanating from Siron, Alma's son Corianton probably rationalized that no harm would come of his liaison with Isabel, but his sinful behavior bore bitter fruit. Why? Because, as Alma so wisely explained, "wickedness never was happiness" (Alma 41:10).

If we are safely sheltered in the embrace of God, we will feel entirely acceptable even though less than whole. None of us has everything, and most of us can hardly do justice to what we do have! Whatever our lack, wherever we don't quite measure up to a standard imposed by ourselves or others, whenever we are unable to make the hoped-for grade, our Redeemer can step in to assist with just the right amount of loving justification to make us feel well about our condition. If we seek Him, He will give us adequate patience to endure the limitations of our current status. Upon request, He will reveal to us the tailored suit of deficiencies and weaknesses fitted to our earthly mission and designed to humble us against self-inflation. Consider how He describes himself: "Behold . . . saith the Lord your God, even Jesus Christ, your

Consider the Lilies, Simon Dewey

advocate, who knoweth the weakness of man and how to succor them who are tempted" (Doctrine & Covenants 62:1).

None is whole save Jesus only. But even He "received not of the fulness at the first, but received grace for grace" (Doctrine & Covenants 93:12), and "grew up" until He "waxed strong" (JST Matthew 3:24). His injunction that we be perfect is meant to motivate us and inspire faith and trust in Him, not to rub our noses in the obvious fact that we are not. As we receive His embrace, there will come a sense that the altitude of our personal orbit was foreordained by a Father who knows the end from the beginning and that the apogee of our earth life will never exceed the circumference of His encircling arms.

THE INVITATION

The art of embracing is so comprehensive it even transcends the need for physical contact. A hug is a hug, even if there's no touching involved. We can embrace with our eyes, enfold with a few words, and clasp with a moment of sincere interest. Simply by paying sincere heed to another person, she or he will feel embraced and held. A physical hug would be inappropriate and unwelcome in many situations, but it is rare that rapt attention would be rejected by one who is attempting to connect without literally connecting. A warm exchange of intellect or an honest acknowledgment of worth can be fulfilling, even without any sharing of body heat.

A friend of mine likes to take photographs of special times and then send copies to those who shared the experience. Every time the recipient looks at the photos, he is once again embraced by the special and sometimes sacred feelings of that moment. The photographer's accompanying greeting adds to the warmth of the gift.

As I travel, I inevitably find tucked away in the recesses of my luggage, notes of love and appreciation hidden there by my wife. They might be clever and bring a smile or thoughtful and touch my heart. Each one is precious, providing a long-distance hug.

We can proffer an embrace by sending a note, lending a listening ear, or accepting an invitation. But it does require a minimal level of sensitivity to the needs of others to make it work. At the risk of some personal embarrassment, I will share an experience in which I failed to have what it took and so lost the privilege of embracing another.

I think I knew it was coming—an invitation to the high-school dance. This dance was designated a girl-ask-boy affair. That was probably a good idea because there were some wonderful girls in our school who deserved to have a special night out but who were seldom invited to the events that did not call for a reversal in the usual gender roles. The young lady who was looking my way was one of them.

I honestly cannot remember her name, but I recall that she sat behind me and a few rows over in English class. Though not unattractive, she was not the prettiest girl in school. She was bright, pleasant, and creative and went out of her way to be friendly with me, but I never responded in more than a casual manner. As the date of the dance approached, however, something or someone tipped me off that she was going to invite me to go with her. This I could not do.

Have you ever looked back and wondered what made you act so unkindly in a situation gone by? Be it teenage foolishness, selfish thoughtlessness, or whatever, I still cannot fathom what caused me to react to her as I did.

After class one day, this young woman sought me out and handed me an envelope. She was her usual friendly self. I was in my usual less-than-responsive mode. The envelope was made of parchment, and my name was beautifully written on it in exquisite calligraphy. I was unimpressed, even a bit embarrassed, and I accepted the envelope and beat a hasty retreat down the hall.

When the envelope was opened, and the winner revealed, I was named, but felt like anything but a victor. In fact, a wave of irrational aversion swept over me. Inside the neatly folded parchment container was another sheet of the same elegant paper, filled with the same fine calligraphy. It was a long and well-written poem, which described her desire to go with me to the dance. I was overwhelmed, but not in the manner anticipated by the artist and poet who had put so much effort into her carefully crafted invitation. Just the opposite. Instead of being pleased, I was completely put off and immediately determined to turn down the invitation. There was nothing to be gained in going to the dance with her. No, the thought of that was not to be considered. And there was no sense being honest about it. At the next opportunity, I would simply tell her that I was going to be out of town and couldn't go to the dance.

The next day, sitting in English class, I could see her out of the corner of my eye in her regular seat. She seemed to be in her typical happy mood, perhaps anticipating a positive response from me. No such luck. Little did she know that she was dealing with a guy whose heart had unfortunately been left at the classroom door, or in his locker, or somewhere, but was certainly not where it should have been.

After class, I approached her with a contrived look of profound disappointment and expressed my dishonest regrets at not being able to go to the dance with her. Her pleasant personality never missed a beat, and if her feelings were hurt, her eyes never gave it away. She smiled and said she understood and that was that. She clutched her notebook and walked away with a girlfriend, and I, with a feeling of foolish relief, headed in the opposite direction. The matter was closed.

Yes, it was over. I wouldn't have to take her to the dance and endure a night of good company, fine food, and fun. I wouldn't have to come off my high horse and exercise a particle of human kindness and unselfishness by going out with someone who wasn't the belle of the ball. It was over, but I have never forgotten.

To this day, I can still see the practiced penmanship on that specially selected paper. And I cringe to think that I was not nice enough to respond in an equally generous way. Instead of creating a nice memory and building what would undoubtedly have been an undemanding friendship, I figured that she was simply not worth the investment of my time. Nearly forty years have passed since that teenage experience. She has certainly forgotten about it. Why should she remember such a thing? But for me, the memory of my graceless, immature response still lingers.

Of course, the real guilt is gone, and I don't continue to beat myself up over it. I was, after all, only a silly, 16-year-old boy and had no intention of hurting her. I simply wasn't emotionally capable at that point of properly handling what for me was an awkward social situation. But I keep the memory alive in order to recall what I might have done and what might have resulted if I had only been willing to accept such a kind invitation. I don't want to forget that it doesn't take much personal sacrifice to make people happy, that a little reaching out, a bit of inclusiveness, never hurts and will likely do a lot of good, for us as well as the recipient of our minor benevolence.

I didn't save that parchment poem. It never became a keepsake. It is, however, framed in the recesses of my memory as a permanent reminder of the importance of acting kindly and with graciousness toward all who may seek what little I have to offer. Wherever you are, classmate, I apologize. I know better now, and I'm sorry we didn't go to the dance together. Hopefully, we can both take comfort in knowing that I have tried since to make up for that poor behavior by embracing, with never a regret, equally generous invitations.

The Girl/Boy of My Dreams

Of those we need to embrace, none is more important than our spouse. Though our spouse may not be fully conscious of her need for such acceptance and comfort, such a yearning is deeply imbedded and its fullfillment is vital to her well-being and self-confidence and to the strength of the relationship. Hugs bring comfort and assurance. We anticipate from our very youth that the one we love will embrace us and we will be one.

Boys and girls are dreamers. They love to look around, discern what is interesting and desirable, and forecast into the future how such things might come into their own lives. Generally speaking, a boy is especially taken by men who work in exciting professions. Boys dream of being pilots, firefighters, policemen, and cowboys. Often, in addition to professional yearnings, a girl is particularly impressed by women who seem to have achieved an enviable level of romance in their lives. She longs to be the subject of a wonderful man's adoration. She dreams of being swept off her feet by a knight in shining armor who will ride into her life with promises of devotion, protection, tenderness, and faithful companionship. While the boys are looking for the thrill of a lifetime, the girls yearn for a lifetime of thrills.

I still see in my wife a lot of that once dreamy-eyed little girl and can imagine her as she was in her early years. She must have noticed the young couples holding hands and wooing one another and wondered about the boy who would someday see her as the prettiest girl in the world and the only one for him. She surely saw the lovely brides and pictured the glory of her own wedding day, joined in holy union and mutual adoration for ever and ever with the man of her dreams. She no doubt observed the young mothers and pictured herself sharing the joys of parenthood with the righteous and compassionate father of her children.

In this exalted vision of life's possibilities, she did not seriously contemplate the likelihood of anything happening to mar her dream. She did not plan on her husband being thoughtless or selfish or unkind. She never perceived the eventuality that she would be angry with her mate or wonder, if only for a moment, if her marriage had been a mistake. She never dreamt of the occasional agonies of parenting or the loneliness and fear and pain that can enter into even the most functional relationships.

As a husband, one of my sacred obligations is to minimize, insomuch as possible, the introduction of the vicissitudes of life into my wife's world and to mitigate the consequences of such when they cannot be avoided. This is a covenant obligation; it is my solemn duty, and also my great pleasure, to do all I can to ensure that the dreams of that little girl, grown to womanhood and flowering in motherhood, are fulfilled.

And remember, she wasn't dreaming so much of the castle as she was of the knight. I may not be able to provide her the lifestyle of a queen, but I can most certainly treat her like one. I can respect her wishes, open the door for her, allow her first choice, sit with her, listen to her, look into her eyes, hold her, and give her the love she has anticipated. I can care for her feelings as tenderly as if they were my own and freely apologize when I tread unkindly. I can pitch in and help her with the "woman's work." I can leave her a note of encouragement when she is down or a message of appreciation for everyday efforts. I can support her in her pursuit of education and self-development. What she wants and needs from me has little to do with our financial success or worldly possessions. In fact, most of what she desires and deserves from me is free. It is to embrace her fully as a unique and wonderful human being.

Of course, the same holds true for her with regard to my hopes and dreams. My wife has a covenant obligation to support and embrace me in becoming all I can, in living up to my potential, in achieving some measure of success in the world, and enjoying the fruits of happiness and contentment in life. She bears a huge burden of responsibility to see that the love she longs to receive is offered in return. She must make an effort to treat me like a conquering hero when I come home from work, show her appreciation for what I do to provide for her and our children, and tender the sweetness that will counter the stresses of my daily toil.

Naturally, a great deal of patience must be exercised in all of this. No one is perfect at it. None of us gets it right every time. The kind word, the loving glance, or the warm embrace may not always come when we want or need them most. But to put forth the effort, to be determined to nourish the dream and keep it alive—that has secured for us a level of joy greater than either of us had even imagined.

I recall the thrill I experienced the first time I ever held my future wife's hand. We were riding together on a bus in Puerto Rico (it's a long story!). Since then, we have held hands many times. We have also locked arms and formed a team. You might call it a "dream team"—working together, still hand in hand, striving to fulfill one another's dreams individually, as a couple, and as a family, enjoying the full embrace of our love. Ideally, I hold her, she holds me, and the Savior holds both of us.

To Those with Empty Arms

C lose companionship is one of the most sweet and satisfying aspects of human existence. A few people seem to have little need for consistent interaction with their fellow beings. They appear to live alone in the wilderness of their own lives without what they would consider to be interference by others. But most of us enjoy the company of other people and, though we also have need for adequate personal space and time, we find great joy in the hours shared in work and play with the members of our family, friends, and our close associates. As previously described, in no relationship is this more fully realized than in the intimate synergy of a good marriage.

It is difficult, then, for those of us who do not enjoy the blessing of being married, to be deprived of this fundamental need to be wholly embraced by another. Life can be cold when arms are empty and hugs are few.

I am acquainted with an outstanding woman who has never married but who has nevertheless created for herself a life filled with rewarding, sweet, and wholesome relationships. I do not know how many lonely, midnight hours she may have spent lamenting her singleness, but her days are filled with selfless caring and service, through which she has accumulated an army of grateful friends and admirers. I do not know what anguish she may have experienced in her private moments of reflection over never having found a husband, but she constantly testifies of the happiness, warmth, and comfort she has found in the loving arms of the Savior. As so many have demonstrated, a single life, filled with service, kindness, and love for people, can be a rich and fulfilling life. It would be a mistake to think otherwise.

But what of physical intimacy? For single people the issue may not be easy to resolve, since without marriage there is no divinely sanctioned means for expressing deeply rooted intimate longings. Those who do not marry, or who do and later become single again, and those with same gender attraction who understand the Lord's plan of happiness are expected to refrain from sexual relations and to walk the uneven path of the worthy celibate.

The focus should not be on whether we can or cannot share with another person the warmth of an intimate embrace, but on what our circumstances will allow us to do and still please God. He should be our focus, as He is our enabler and our reason for being. Regardless of what He asks us to overcome or what He expects us to give, we must be prepared to respond with total commitment to Him. Encircled in the arms of His love, fully surrendering to His embrace, we will be able to serve, sacrifice, and be satisfied. In the process, compensating joys will present themselves, and we can avoid feelings of waste and want.

Chastity, like charity, is a universal commandment. We cannot expect exemptions, but we can seek redemption in the arms of the One who knows us to the core and loves us regardless of the burdens we carry. In reality, He carried them before He gave them to us. Somehow He knows how heavy they are, how "hard to bear." So we willingly take His yoke upon us and move on, our load lightened by His sharing the burden and the assurance we have of His everlasting concern and unfailing affection. God bless the virtuous, uncomplaining, single person who knows the embrace of Jesus.

Such feelings of noble sentiment may be more difficult to come by, however, for the one who is married, who ought to be enjoying the embrace of a good companion, but is not. There are no tears as bitter as those that flow from the eyes of a neglected or rejected spouse. No failure is more painful than that associated with the failure of a once hopeful marriage. Shattered dreams, fear for the future, and grave concern for children amplify the disappointment of trust betrayed. Loneliness, anger, and frustration are magnified through long, sleepless nights, spent in a desperate search for answers to questions that could easily have been found in a healing embrace. And all of this is made even harder by the knowledge that such problems could have been avoided had loving arms been offered and received early on. It's tough to give a hug when your back is turned.

In such grievous circumstances we must look to the One who will rekindle our hope and reignite our will to carry on. We may do our seeking on bended knee with hands folded and head bowed, awaiting the inspiration of God. We might search Him out in the scriptures and other good books, led by the Spirit as our eyes scan the pages for new thoughts and ideas for coping to be discovered in His word. He may be found in the support of extended family, the understanding of friends, the insight of counselors, and the unconditional love of children. He may send His embrace through inspiring music, a beautiful sunset, or a

Jesus Knocking at the Door, Del Parson

fragrant flower. He can manifest Himself in such ways and many, many more.

"Ask, and it shall be given you; seek, and ye shall find; knock, and it shall be opened unto you" (Matthew 7:7). On the other side of the door of your beseeching He waits to answer in His own way and time. "And then, if thou endure it well" (Doctrine & Covenants 121:8), He will come into your heart and into your mind and you will feel the relief of His love and the healing comfort of His acceptance. He will guide you and you will be empowered with strength to make up for the shortfall in your mate's devotion. The agony of a cold companionship or no companionship at all can be mitigated by the warm embrace of the Master.

THE EMBRACE OF JESUS

Available to all, free of charge, and there for the asking is the loving embrace of our Savior Jesus Christ. To Him we can turn at any time, in any place, regardless of all negative considerations. The only qualifying factor is our willingness to "ask with a sincere heart, with real intent, having faith in Christ" (Moroni 10:4). He will then reach out to us through His Spirit in a manner suited to our needs and hold us to His bosom as a rescuing Shepherd. We will feel the tenderness of His acceptance, the warmth of His love, and the relief of His deliverance.

The depths of human sorrow cannot take us so low that He is not there to attend. Nor are there heights to which He cannot ascend. There are no imaginations of the mind, no calculations of the heart, that He cannot sort through and understand.

Consider the rhetorical question of the Psalmist:

"Whither shall I go from thy spirit? or whither shall I flee from thy presence? If I ascend up into heaven, thou art there: if I make my bed in hell, behold, thou art there. If I take the wings of the morning, and dwell in the uttermost parts of the sea; Even there shall thy hand lead me, and thy right hand shall hold me" (Psalm 139:7–10).

Along with Lehi, I testify He will hold you. "Behold, the Lord hath redeemed my soul from hell; I have beheld his glory, and I am encircled about eternally in the arms of his love" (2 Nephi 1:15).

I know you can feel the arms of His love.

In the earliest days of the Restoration, the faith of the brethren and sisters was built upon a rather thin store of doctrine and experience. In their spiritual infancy the Saints needed and received the frequent and personal assurance of a loving Savior as they encountered the obstacles of doubt that must have loomed in their path from time to time. Not just doubt in the cause, but doubt in their ability to meet its demands. At what may have been such a time, the Lord spoke to Oliver Cowdrey.

"Behold, thou art Oliver, and I have spoken unto thee because of thy desires; therefore treasure up these words in thy heart. Be faithful and diligent in keeping the commandments of God, and I will encircle thee in the arms of my love" (Doctrine & Covenants 6:20).

And the Lord didn't speak just to Oliver, but to you and me, also. Read that verse again and this time insert your own name in the place of Oliver's. Believe it all applies to you as well. I know it does.

"Behold, thou art [your name], and I have spoken unto thee because of thy desires; therefore treasure up these words in thy heart. Be faithful and diligent in keeping the commandments of God, and I will encircle thee in the arms of my love."

That is our promise! We see it literally fulfilled in what is perhaps the most tender moment in all scripture. It occurs in the Garden Tomb following the death and resurrection of Jesus. His three-day mission across the veil had been completed, and He was nearly ready, it seems, to return to His Father to report the efforts of His beneficent ministry among the children of men on both sides of the veil. One thing He had yet to do—confirm to His earthly followers that He is not dead, but is risen, as He had promised.

The account of John the Beloved:

"But Mary stood without at the sepulchre weeping: and as she wept, she stooped down, and looked into the sepulchre, And seeth two angels in white sitting, the one at the head, and the other at the feet, where the body of Jesus had lain. And they say unto her, Woman, why weepest thou? She saith unto them, Because they have taken away my Lord, and I know not where they have laid him. And when she had thus said, she turned herself back, and saw Jesus standing, and knew not that it was Jesus.

"Jesus saith unto her, Woman, why weepest thou? whom seekest thou? She, supposing him to be the gardener, saith unto him, Sir, if thou have borne him hence, tell me where thou hast laid him, and I will take him away.

Why Weepest Thou, Simon Dewey

"Jesus saith unto her, Mary. She turned herself, and saith unto him, Rabboni; which is to say, Master.

"Jesus saith unto her, Touch me not; for I am not yet ascended to my Father: but go to my brethren, and say unto them, I ascend unto my Father, and your Father; and to my God, and your God" (John 20:11–17).

Hearing one word, her name, Mary was able to turn from her nearly overwhelming grief and receive the Savior once again. Thus came another instantaneous and miraculous healing. Mary's empty heart was filled, her desperate mind was calmed, and her love was renewed to overflowing.

But our insight into this sacred moment is made all the more meaningful by the Prophet Joseph Smith and his correction of the text. He changed one word. In his inspired translation of verse seventeen he replaced the word *touch* with the word *hold*.

"*Hold* me not; for I am not yet ascended to my Father" (JST John 20:17; emphasis added).

Joseph corrected the noble compilers of the King James Version, who had rendered a mistranslation of the Greek verb *haptomai*. In the Greek, *haptomai* is *not* "to touch," but "to embrace." In addition, His request was *not* necessarily intended to stop her from embracing Him. It is possible He may have been asking her to break off her embrace. The injunction of Jesus to Mary may not have been a command to leave Him alone, not to touch Him. Perhaps it was a sweet reminder that her tender embrace needed to end so that He could depart to complete His work. It is not unlikely that He had warmly embraced his dear friend and companion and that He was simply suggesting to her that His time with her had come to an end for the moment.

The Savior is never untouchable, but is ever available to all who will reach out to Him to be enfolded in His embrace. Surely He extended His arms to Mary. Surely He held her, embraced her, as the writer of the original Greek intended us to know. Surely if we call upon Him He will respond with our name and we will be "encircled about eternally in the arms of his love" (2 Nephi 1:15).

And remember, "eternally" goes both ways—

forward and back. It means we have been and we can always be encircled in the arms of His love. Again: "Behold, thou art [*your name*], and I have spoken unto thee because of thy desires; therefore treasure up these words in thy heart. Be faithful and diligent in keeping the commandments of God, and I will encircle thee in the arms of my love" (Doctrine & Covenants 6:20).

He says to us what He could not yet say to Mary at the Garden Tomb. To us He implores, *haptomai*— "hold Me, detain Me, keep Me, and let Me embrace you—for I *have* ascended to my Father, and your Father; and to my God, and your God. I have descended below all things and ascended above all things for your sake" (see Doctrine & Covenants 88:6).

Even *your* sake. He did it for each of us, but you must reach beyond a sense of the infinity of the Atonement to accept the portion thereof intended for you and you alone. You have the privilege of His embrace. He is not on the cross. He is not in the tomb. He stands looking upon you, asking, "Whom seekest thou?" He whispers your name and waits for you to recognize Him. He wants you to feel His embrace.

So, yield to His entreaty. Give in to His love and, please, please say to the Savior, "Just hold me. Tighter."

> *God be with you till we meet again;*
> *By his counsels guide, uphold you;*
> *With his sheep securely fold you.*
> *God be with you till we meet again. . . .*
> *When life's perils thick confound you,*
> *Put his arms unfailing round you.*
> *God be with you till we meet again.*
> (Hymns, no. 152)